CHARLES D

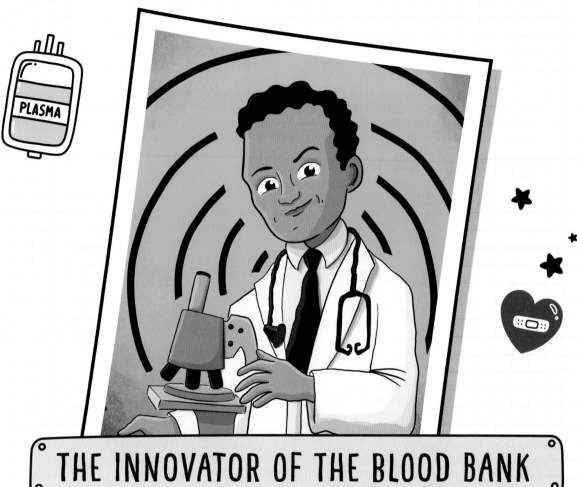

THE INNOVATOR OF THE BLOOD BANK

By Aaron Talley

Illustrated by Subi Bosa

Children's Press®
An imprint of Scholastic Inc.

Special thanks to our consultant Rhea Sylvia Drew Ivie, daughter of Charles Drew, for her insight into the life and work of her father.

Special thanks also to our medical content consultant, Eloi Montañez Miralles, associate professor, Department of Physiological Sciences, Faculty of Medicine and Health Sciences at the University of Barcelona.

Library of Congress Cataloging-in-Publication Data
Names: Talley, Aaron, author. | Bosa, Subi, illustrator.
Title: Charles Drew: The innovator of the blood bank / by Aaron Talley; illustrated by Subi Bosa.
Description: First edition. | New York, NY: Children's Press, an imprint of Scholastic Inc., 2023. | Series: Bright minds | Includes bibliographical references and index. | Audience: Ages 8–10. | Audience: Grades 4–6. | Summary: "A biography series highlighting the work and social impact of BIPOC inventors"—Provided by publisher.
Identifiers: LCCN 2022028659 (print) | LCCN 2022028660 (ebook) | ISBN 9781338865349 (library binding) | ISBN 9781338865356 (paperback) | ISBN 9781338865363 (ebook)
Subjects: LCSH: Drew, Charles, 1904–1950—Juvenile literature. | Surgeons—United States—Biography—Juvenile literature. | African American surgeons—United States—Biography—Juvenile literature. | Blood banks—United States—Juvenile literature. | BISAC: JUVENILE NONFICTION / Biography & Autobiography / General | JUVENILE NONFICTION / Technology / Inventions | LCGFT: Biographies.
Classification: LCC RD27.35.D74 T345 2023 (print) | LCC RD27.35.D74 (ebook) | DDC 617.092 [B]—dc23/eng/20220711
LC record available at https://lccn.loc.gov/2022028659
LC ebook record available at https://lccn.loc.gov/2022028660

10 9 8 7 6 5 4 3 2 1   23 24 25 26 27

Printed in China   62
First edition, 2023

Book design by Kathleen Petelinsek
Book prototype design by Maria Bergós / Book&Look

Photos ©: 5 center: Alfred Eisenstaedt/The LIFE Picture Collection/Shutterstock; 6 top right: Courtesy of the Moorland-Spingarn Research Center/National Library of Medicine; 6 map: Elisa Lara/Dreamstime; 7 top: Everett/Shutterstock; 8 bottom right, 9 bottom left, 10 bottom, 11 bottom: Courtesy of the Moorland-Spingarn Research Center/National Library of Medicine; 12 center right: Amherst College Archives and Special Collections/Courtesy of the Moorland-Spingarn Research Center/National Library of Medicine; 13 center left: Lebrecht History/Bridgeman Images; 13 bottom right: Howard University. Moorland-Spingarn Research Center. Charles R. Drew Papers/National Library of Medicine; 15 bottom left: Courtesy of the Moorland-Spingarn Research Center/National Library of Medicine; 17 bottom right: Howard University/ Moorland-Spingarn Research Center/National Library of Medicine; 18 top right: Harris & Ewing/Library of Congress; 19 bottom center: Rev. Jared Waterbury Scudder's Photos/Geni; 23 bottom left: Courtesy of the Moorland-Spingarn Research Center/National Library of Medicine; 25 bottom left: Keystone/Hulton Archive/Getty Images; 26 bottom left, 27 bottom right, 28 center right : Courtesy of the Moorland-Spingarn Research Center/National Library of Medicine; 31 top right: Patrick G. Jordan/HMdb.org; 32 top right: Courtesy CDU; 32 center: Courtesy Arlington Public Library; 32 bottom right: Slowking4/Wikimedia; 33 top right: Scurlock Studio Records/Archives Center/National Museum of American History/Behring Center/Smithsonian Institution/National Library of Medicine.

All other photos © Designed by Freepik and Shutterstock.

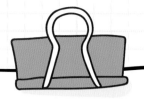

TABLE OF CONTENTS

★★★★

LET'S POKE INTO...

Charles Drew was fascinated by blood. (Don't worry, he wasn't a vampire!)

Charles Drew was a smart and **courageous** doctor. One of the greatest of all time.

He is famous for improving the **blood bank**. Yep . . . you read that right. A bank, but instead of money, it stores blood! (Now, a vampire would really get a kick out of that.)

I don't drink blood! I study it!

...THE STORY OF CHARLES DREW

Every year, about seven million people around the world donate blood. People who donate blood are called **donors**. Blood banks can store their blood so it can be used to help sick people.

Before Charles Drew, storing blood was complicated and sometimes dangerous. But his discoveries taught us how to use stored blood longer and more safely. It helped doctors and nurses save millions of lives every year.

I am the innovator of the blood bank!

To learn more about this fascinating scientist, let's poke into the story of Charles Drew!

Charles Richard Drew was born on June 3, 1904, in **Washington, DC**.

He married **Minnie Lenore Robbins** on September 23, 1939. They had three daughters (**Bebe Roberta**, **Charlene Rosella**, and **Rhea Sylvia**) and a son (**Charles Richard, Jr.**).

He died on April 1, 1950, in **Burlington, North Carolina**.

Charles Drew with his wife, Lenore, and their four kids

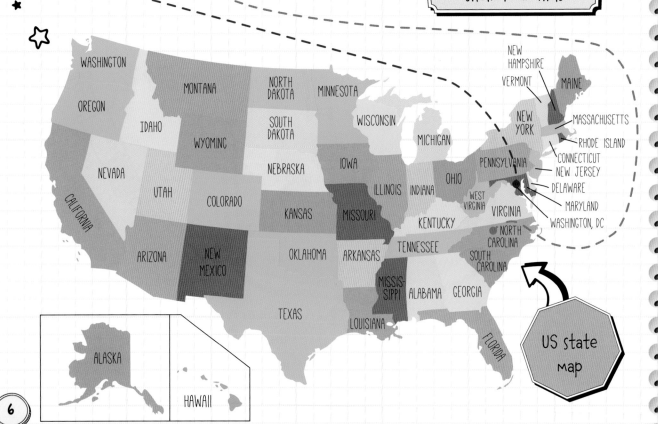

US state map

KNOWN FOR...

- ☑ Being an amazing athlete
- ☑ Becoming a surgeon
- ☑ Teaching young doctors
- ☑ His research on blood
- ☑ Helping to perfect the blood bank
- ☑ Conceiving mobile blood donations with refrigerated **bloodmobiles**
- ☑ Standing up against **racism**

You can do anything you think you can!

Charles Drew believed that, if you worked hard, you could conquer any obstacle and achieve anything you wanted. Exactly like he did!

A HARDWORKING FAMILY

Charles "Charlie" Drew was born in Washington, DC, in a neighborhood with a funny name: Foggy Bottom!

He was the oldest of his four siblings, Joseph, Elsie, Nora, and Eva.

His dad, Richard Drew, was a carpet layer, and his mom, Nora Burrell Drew, was trained to be a teacher, but she never taught. His parents did not have a lot of money. They worked hard for their family and taught Charlie to be responsible and independent.

We love you, Charlie!

Charles with his brother, Joseph, and sisters Elsie and Nora

Charles

Joseph

Eva wasn't born yet!

Nora

Elsie

EXTRA! EXTRA! READ ALL ABOUT IT!

As a boy, Charlie was very **ambitious**. He had a lot of jobs. He worked as a **paperboy**, did construction jobs, and was even a lifeguard.

Extra! Extra! Read all about it!

good news

THE WAY THINGS WERE
When Charlie was young, paperboys used to hand-deliver newspapers to people.

This is Charles when he worked as a lifeguard at Francis Swimming Pool.

He did not always want to be a doctor, though. In high school, he wanted to be an engineer.

SUPERSTAR ATHLETE

Charlie was super smart, but he wasn't the best student.

He put most of his effort into sports. He did swimming, football, basketball, track, and baseball. He was good at all of them! He was an amazing athlete and won many awards for his skills.

What time is practice?

Charles

In high school, he was voted Best Athlete, Most Popular Student, and Student Who Had Done the Most for the School.

Charles Drew with his high school basketball team

A NEW INSPIRATION

Sadly, Charlie's little sister Elsie was very weak from a disease called **tuberculosis**. Before Charlie graduated high school, she passed away from the flu.

He had been really close to his sister. Her death inspired him to become a doctor.

I'm going to be a doctor to help sick people like my sister!

DREW, CHARLES—"Charlie"

"You can do anything you think you can."

Ambitious, popular, athletic, sturdy.
Pres. Class '21; Pres., Athletic Association '21; Pres. Rex Club, '22; Capt. Baseball Team '22; Champion High Jumper; Capt. Co. F; Holder of two Walker Memorial Medals.

Charles Drew's high school yearbook entry.

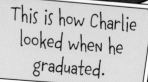

This is how Charlie looked when he graduated.

OUTRUNNING RACISM

When he was eighteen, Charlie was so good at sports that he got a **scholarship** to attend Amherst College in Massachusetts.

In college, Charlie ran track and played football. His skills were *legendary!*

But he faced racial **discrimination** while playing on his college sports teams. Rival teams were often mean to Charlie and his other Black teammates. Even though he was the top player, a white player was selected to be football captain during Charlie's senior year of college. On top of that, some restaurants refused to serve him because he was Black.

He did not let this stop him!

Charles Drew in his football uniform in college. Football uniforms sure looked different back then, didn't they?

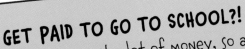

GET PAID TO GO TO SCHOOL?!
College can cost a lot of money, so a scholarship is when you're so talented at school or sports that a school pays you to go there. (Yep, someone can pay YOU to go to school!)

The school had 600 students. Charlie was one of only thirteen Black students.

A SCHOLAR!

After graduating college, Charlie needed to go to medical school to become a doctor.

At the time, Black and white people were racially **segregated**, so Charlie only had a few universities to choose from. Still, he made the best of it.

He chose to go to a school called McGill University in Canada. Most students were white, but they did admit a small number of Black students each year.

At McGill, Charlie was trained as a surgeon, a doctor who specializes in performing operations.

McGill College, Montreal, Que.

McGill University is one of the oldest schools in Montreal, Canada.

Charlie was still an amazing athlete, but this time, he also did really well in his classes. He won many awards for his schoolwork.

This is the 1933 McGill University track team. Charlie is at the center. He led McGill to five track-and-field championships in a row!

A SHOCKING FOCUS

Charlie wanted to know how to help people when their bodies are in **shock**. This is a term used to describe how the body feels when it loses a lot of blood during an accident.

When a person's body is in shock, they feel **queasy** and tired, and they might throw up.

The only way to help a body "in shock" was to replace the blood with a **blood transfusion** from donors.

But in the 1930s, blood transfusions were hard to do. Blood became **contaminated** easily and could only be kept in the fridge for two weeks.

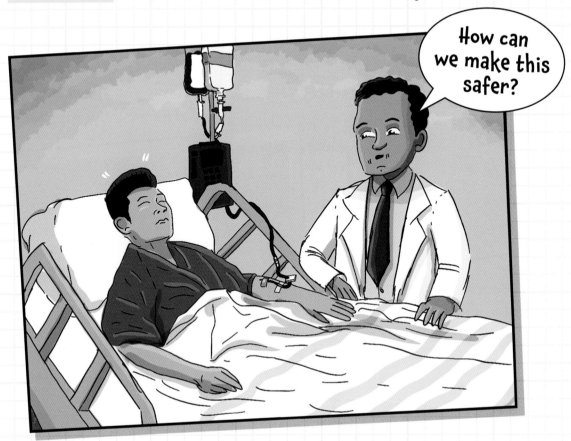

How can we make this safer?

FRESH BLOOD

Charlie knew that if he could improve the way transfusions were done, he would be able to save people who were sick.

ARE YOU MY TYPE?
Did you know there are different blood types? They are labeled A, B, AB, or O. Before doctors share blood between patients, they make sure the type matches. Otherwise, the patient could get sick.

So Charlie worked hard to learn a lot from his professors before graduating from McGill and becoming a doctor.

I think we are a match!

Let me reintroduce myself! You can call me Dr. Drew.

Charles Drew's graduation photo from McGill University

WHAT IS BLOOD ACTUALLY?

Sure, blood just looks red. VERY red. But did you know it's actually made of many different components? Each component has a different job to protect our bodies and keep us healthy.

Red blood **cells** carry oxygen to all the organs in our bodies, like our heart.

White blood cells help us fight infection from outside germs.

Blood also has platelets—small, disc-shaped pieces of cells. When you get a cut, platelets pile on top of one another to keep blood from oozing out! They are where scabs come from.

And then there's plasma! Plasma is a yellowy liquid that carries all the other blood cells around! It's mostly made of water. It is also made up of other nutrients our bodies need, like sugars and vitamins!

The heart pumps blood through tubes in our bodies called veins and arteries.

PLASMA

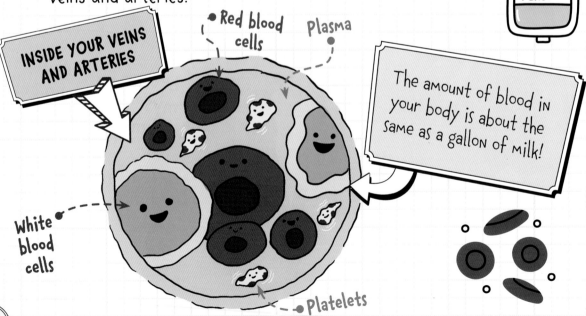

INSIDE YOUR VEINS AND ARTERIES

Red blood cells

Plasma

White blood cells

The amount of blood in your body is about the same as a gallon of milk!

Platelets

MOVIN' ON UP

After graduating from medical school, Dr. Drew went to work at Howard University in Washington, DC.

Howard University is a **Historically Black College or University (HBCU)**. These are schools that were created as a safe place for Black people to go to college.

Charlie knew that going to Howard would allow him to practice his work and feel respected.

He was now officially a doctor. Since he worked at a university, he got to teach as well.

MORE ABOUT HBCUS

HBCUs are still around. Did you know there are more than one hundred of them across the country? Many famous Black people have attended them, including Chadwick Boseman, who played Black Panther, and Kamala Harris, the first Black and female vice president of the United States. They both went to Howard.

Time to show Howard how much I love blood!

Dr. Drew (center) teaches students at Howard University.

17

At Howard, Charlie met a man named **Numa P. G. Adams.** Mr. Adams was the first Black person in charge of the medical school at Howard.

Mr. Adams loved Charles Drew and thought he was very smart. He wrote nice things about him.

A portrait of Numa P. G. Adams

Yes, Charlie. You are a very intelligent and hardworking man.

Many people at Howard loved Charlie!

But after five years, Charlie decided he wanted to go back to school to get his PhD. He loved helping patients. But he also wanted to have lots of time to do research.

His great work at Howard earned him a spot at one of the best medical schools in the country: Columbia University.

THE BEST REPORT CARD EVER

A PhD is the highest **degree** you can get from going to a university. It means you're super smart and have worked very hard at researching.

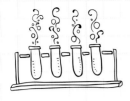

RESEARCHER CHARLIE

At Columbia, Charlie wanted to focus his research on making blood transfusions more **efficient**. He got assigned to work in a lab run by a man named John Scudder.

Black doctors working at Columbia usually only did research. Because of racial discrimination, they were not allowed to work with patients. But Charlie was determined to do both. He had a lot of charm and talent! His impressive skills **convinced** John Scudder and his other bosses to let him work with patients, too.

I am glad you are here.

John Scudder was a big ally in helping Charlie finish his research.

A BETTER BLOOD BANK

Back in the lab, Charlie wanted to figure out how to help other doctors and nurses store blood for longer periods of time. He wanted to make blood banks better.

He first did a *lot* of research:

- ☑ He read all the articles he could find about blood and blood banks.
- ☑ He learned about the history of blood transfusions.
- ☑ He talked to a few doctors who led their own blood transfusion clinics.
- ☑ He learned about the shapes and sizes of containers doctors used to store blood.

✓ He looked at the different temperatures blood had been kept in.

✓ He investigated the types of **preservatives** used to keep blood fresh.

After all his studying . . .

EUREKA!

Charlie started his own blood bank. He used only the best methods he had researched.

And he was able to create the most efficient, organized, and long-lasting blood bank to ever exist.

BLOOD - RED CELLS = GENIUS!

The secret to Charlie's blood bank was a new technique he created to separate the different parts of blood. It was called **centrifuging**. By spinning blood really fast, he was able to separate the heavier parts of blood from the lighter parts. This separated blood into three parts: red blood cells, white blood cells and platelets, and plasma.

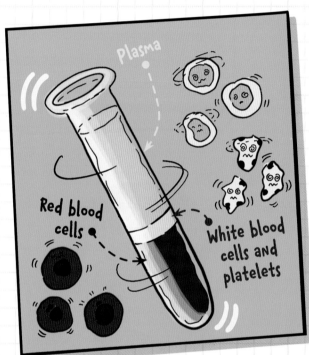

Plasma

Red blood cells

White blood cells and platelets

Charlie had figured out that the red blood cells were what caused blood to spoil in the first place.

So, when plasma was separated from the red cells and other blood components, it could be stored for longer periods of time. Actually, plasma by itself could be stored for up to one year! Charlie figured out how to dry the plasma, store it, and then make it liquid again when it needed to be used.

THE INCREDIBLE QUALITIES OF PLASMA
- It can be stored for longer than "regular" blood.
- It matches any blood type without making someone sick.
- It can be used to treat shock.
- It can be injected into muscles as well as veins.
- It can help save a lot of lives!

PLASMA

22

While Charlie was at Columbia, he attended a medical **conference** in Atlanta, Georgia. There he met a professor from Spelman College, an HBCU attended primarily by Black women. Her name was Minnie. They fell in love, and soon after, they got married.

BABY BEBE
Charles and Minnie named their oldest daughter Bebe. It comes from "blood bank"! (BB—get it?)

Photo of Bebe, Charlie's oldest daughter

GO, CHARLIE, GO!

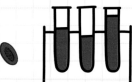

A year after getting married, Charlie graduated from Columbia. He became the first African American to get a doctorate from Columbia's medical school! His work with John Scudder on the blood bank was praised by many people.

Now Charlie was considered an **expert** in his field. And because of his work, blood banks were more useful than ever before.

PAGING DR. DREW!

In 1940, Charlie decided to go back and teach at Howard University.

By then, World War II was **raging** in Europe. A lot of British soldiers were getting hurt in the war. To keep them healthy, Britain needed more blood . . . and more plasma.

So they asked America for help.

America knew just who to put in charge.

WORLD WAR II
World War II started in 1939, when Adolf Hitler, at the time the racist dictator of Germany, decided to invade other neighboring countries. A group of countries including the United States, France, and Great Britain (known as the Allies) teamed up to fight against Adolf Hitler. They won. However, the war lasted six years, and between 35 and 60 million people died. It was one of the most brutal wars in history.

The country of Japan was on Germany's side. They sometimes crashed piloted planes on purpose, as if they were missiles. These were called kamikazes. This photo shows a US ship after it was hit by two kamikazes. A lot of donated blood was needed to help the injured soldiers.

FOLLOW THE LEADER

The project was called Blood for Britain, and Dr. Drew (together with John Scudder), were put in charge of it.

Charlie needed to create the biggest blood bank ever. He knew a lot of lives depended on him. So he decided to teach his new blood-banking techniques to as many doctors and nurses as he could.

Look, it's all in the drying!

Blood Bank

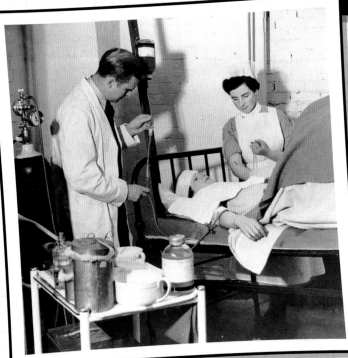

A British victim of an air strike gets a donation of plasma from America.

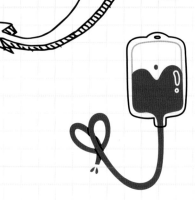

NAILED IT!

He set up blood banks all over New York City. He also sent trucks filled with refrigerators outside the city to get blood from more donors.

The blood received was centrifuged. The plasma was dried. Charlie made sure the plasma was not contaminated. Then it was shipped to England.

By the end of the project, Charlie had helped collect almost 15,000 blood donations and ship the equivalent of 1,300 gallons of plasma to England. (That's like 1,300 milk jugs full of blood!)

People celebrated him for managing such a big effort.

With some help from Charlie, Britain and its allies won World War II.

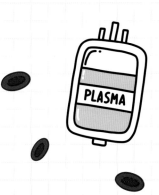

PLASMA

The British military was very happy with the plasma from Dr. Drew's efforts!

BLOODMOBILES!

Charlie became world-famous for his blood bank efforts.

Soon, a major organization, the American Red Cross, asked him to set up a national blood bank. This would be his biggest blood bank yet.

To carry it out, he came up with the idea of refrigerated bloodmobiles. These were vehicles that helped get blood donations on the go. Now people could give blood regardless of where they lived. The project was a success.

THAT'S A LOT OF BLOOD!
Refrigerated bloodmobiles are still around today. They can collect up to 1,000 gallons of blood a year.

You really took this blood thing far, huh?

Jealous?

Donate Blood on the BLOODMOBILE

Charles Drew stands outside of the bloodmobile. This was the first time anyone had seen anything like this!

BOO TO RACISM

Unfortunately, at first, the American Red Cross didn't allow Black people to donate blood. They believed many white people would prefer not to receive blood from a Black person.

Isn't that strange?

Many organizations protested against this. They knew it was wrong! Charlie disagreed with this as well. He was the blood expert, after all. He knew that somebody's race had nothing to do with their blood.

As a result, in January 1942, Black people were allowed to donate blood. But the Red Cross still kept it separate from blood donated by white people. Dr. Drew later spoke out against this, too.

RUMOR ALERT: PART ONE

Dr. Drew left the Red Cross after a year. Some people believe it was because of the blood segregation policy. But NO ONE is sure. He had always planned to return to Howard University, and he likely wanted to spend more time with his family.

There is no scientific evidence of any difference between blood of different races.

THE TOP DOC

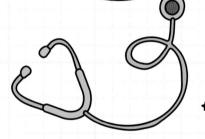

Afterward, Charlie continued to shine.

He became the top professor of surgery at Howard University. He loved this because he got the opportunity to train more young Black doctors. Many of his students got top scores on their tests.

He even became the first Black **examiner** for the American Board of Surgery. Who were the best surgeons in the country? Now it was Charlie's job to decide this.

MOST IMPORTANT
Charles Drew accomplished a lot of things during his lifetime. But the one he was most proud of was teaching young doctors.

A TRAGIC END

On April 1, 1950, Charlie was on his way to help out at a clinic in Tuskegee, Alabama, when he had a car accident. He fell asleep at the wheel near Burlington, North Carolina, and his car spun off the road.

He was rushed to the hospital, where doctors had to do a blood transfusion. They had to use some of the same techniques Charlie had helped perfect.

Sadly, he still passed away. His injuries were too severe.

RUMOR ALERT: PART TWO

There was a rumor that Charlie wasn't treated fairly at the hospital due to his race. But it's not true. The doctors taking care of him said everything possible was done to help him live.

In 1986, a memorial was dedicated to Dr. Drew near Haw Road, North Carolina. This is the spot where he was unfortunately killed. More than 300 people, including Charlie's family, attended the event.

In loving memory of Charles Drew

Charles Drew was an amazing doctor and teacher. So amazing that there are over fifty health centers and schools named after him all around the United States. One of them is Charles R. Drew University in Los Angeles, California.

Charles R. Drew University is also an HBCU!

This is the house where Charlie lived with his family.

There are also many buildings named after him in his hometown of Washington, DC. This includes a building at Howard University, the HBCU where he did a lot of his work.

And if you ever go to Arlington, Virginia, you can see his house! It's considered a national landmark.

This marker outside of Charlie's old home tells you about his life!

THE NEXT CHARLES DREW?

Charles Drew's intelligence and courage helped save so many lives. And he did so while fighting against racism.

> Charlie at his desk later in his life

Maybe one day you'll be a top surgeon or a medical researcher, and you will help people just like he did! If you do, smile and be proud as you think of Charles Drew.

He was the Innovator of the Blood Bank. And so much more!

WOULD YOU DONATE BLOOD?
About 4.5 million Americans need blood each year. So if you donate blood, you'll be helping a lot of people out. You can donate when you turn seventeen years old. Do you think you will do it?

YOUR TURN!

Charles Drew didn't invent the blood bank, but he did a lot of the work to make it better. Many inventions are actually improvements on earlier inventions. Now it is your turn!

Pick something that already exists. It can be your favorite toy, game, or gadget. Learn as much as you can about your item.

Then answer the following questions:

When was it made?

How was it made?

What problem was it trying to solve?

What changes have been made to it over time?

What company sells the item now?

Now ask yourself these questions:

How could I make this item better?

What would I change about it? Why?

What would I keep the same? Why?

How could I make more people happy with this item?

Be as creative as you can.

To finish, write a pretend letter to the company that makes the item. Explain how you would improve it.

GLOSSARY

ambitious (am-BISH-uhs) having a strong desire and will to succeed

blood bank (bluhd bangk) a place where blood is donated and stored

bloodmobiles (BLUHD-moh-beelz) vehicles staffed and equipped for collecting blood from donors

blood transfusion (bluhd trans-FYOO-zhuhn) the injection of blood from one person into the body of someone else who is injured or sick

cells (selz) the smallest units of an animal or a plant

centrifuging (sen-TRIF-yuh-jing) moving or tending to move away from the center

conference (KAHN-fur-uhns) a formal meeting for discussion

contaminated (kuhn-TAM-uh-nay-tid) containing harmful or undesirable substances

convinced (kuhn-VINST) having persuaded someone to do or believe something

courageous (kuh-RAY-juhs) brave; being able to do something that is scary

degree (di-GREE) a title given by a college or university, as in a degree in medicine

discrimination (dis-krim-i-NAY-shuhn) prejudice or unfair behavior toward others based on differences in such things as age, race, or gender

donor (DOH-nur) someone who agrees to give his or her body, or a part of it (for example, blood), to medical science to help sick people

efficient (i-FISH-uhnt) working very well and not wasting time or energy

examiner (ig-ZAM-in-ur) a person whose job is to inspect something; an inspector

expert (EK-spurt) someone who has a special skill or knows a lot about a particular subject

paperboy (PAY-pur-boi) a boy who delivers newspapers to people's homes

preservatives (pri-ZUR-vuh-tivs) substances used to preserve an item, especially a chemical used to keep food from spoiling

queasy (KWEE-zee) sick to your stomach or nauseated

racism (RAY-si-zuhm) the belief that a particular race is better than others; treating people unfairly or cruelly because of their race

raging (RAYJ-ing) happening with great force

scholarship (SKAH-lur-ship) money given to pay for someone to go to college or to follow a course of study

segregation (seg-ri-GAY-shuhn) the act or practice of keeping people or groups apart, as in racial segregation

shock (shahk) a medical condition caused by a serious drop in blood pressure, sometimes causing loss of consciousness; shock may be caused by severe injury or great emotional upset

tuberculosis (tu-bur-kyuh-LOH-sis) a highly contagious disease caused by bacteria that usually affects the lungs

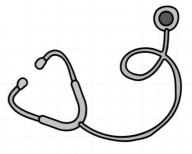

INDEX

FURTHER READING

Graham, Ian. *The Science of Scabs and Pus: The Sticky Truth about Blood.* New York: Scholastic Inc., 2017.

Schraff, Anne E. *The Life of Dr. Charles Drew: Blood Bank Innovator.* New Jersey: Enslow Publishers, Inc., 2014.

Venezia, Mike. *Charles Drew: Doctor Who Got the World Pumped Up to Donate Blood.* New York: Scholastic Inc., 2009.

Whitehurst, Susan. *Dr. Charles Drew, Medical Pioneer.* Colorado: The Child's World, 2001.

Read the other books in this series:

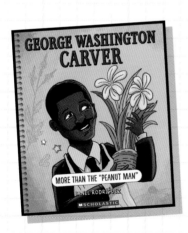

ABOUT THE AUTHOR

Aaron Talley is a teacher and a writer who lives in Chicago, Illinois. Like Charles Drew, he loves to inspire his students and all kids everywhere to follow their passions! He is originally from Detroit, Michigan.

ABOUT THE ILLUSTRATOR

As a child, Subi Bosa drew pictures all the time, in every room of the house—sometimes even on the walls! His mother always told everyone, "He knew how to draw before he could properly hold a pencil." Today, Subi continues to draw fun picture books, comics, and graphic novels from his home in Cape Town, a city in South Africa. He has won many awards for his work!